BORN TO SHOP © and ® 2006 History & Heraldry Ltd.
All rights reserved.

This edition published by Ravette Publishing 2006.

Printed and bound in Belgium

ISBN 10: 1-84161-255-3
ISBN 13: 978-1-84161-255-3

ЯR
RAVETTE PUBLISHING

Good morning...

let the stress

begin

I
don't
do
mornings

You can touch
the dust,
but please don't
write in it

Many people have
eaten in this kitchen
and have gone
on to live normal
healthy lives

We child-proofed
the house,
but they keep
finding their
way in

Sometimes I wake up grumpy, and sometimes I let him sleep

Hard work pays off
in the future,
laziness
pays off
now

So it's
not home
sweet
home ...
adjust!

I understand the concepts of cooking and cleaning, just not how they apply to me

This is a
self-cleaning kitchen,
so clean up after
yourself

I can only
please one person
per day.
Today is
not your day.

At my age
a soak
in the tub
is just a wild
night in

I kiss

better

than

I Cook

I'm usually gorgeous, but it's my day off

Whenever I get the
urge to exercise,
I lie down
until the feeling
passes

It's been
Monday
all week

Some days are just a **total** waste of make-up

I do not

suffer from

stress,

but I am a

carrier

Other BORN TO SHOP titles available ...

	ISBN	Price
All men are created equal... equally useless	1 84161 257 X	£4.99
I never met a calorie I didn't like	1 84161 256 1	£4.99
Friends are the family we choose for ourselves	1 84161 254 5	£4.99

HOW TO ORDER   Please send a cheque/postal order in £ sterling, made payable to 'Ravette Publishing' for the cover price of the books and allow the following for post & packaging ...

UK & BFPO	70p for the first book & 40p per book thereafter
Europe & Eire	£1.30 for the first book & 70p per book thereafter
Rest of the world	£2.20 for the first book & £1.10 per book thereafter

RAVETTE PUBLISHING LTD
Unit 3 Tristar Centre
Star Road
Partridge Green
West Sussex RH13 8RA
Tel: 01403 711443   Fax: 01403 711554   Email: ravettepub@aol.com

Prices and availability are subject to change without prior notice.